Gravity

Lynne Schmidt

Published by Nightingale & Sparrow Press, 2019

Cover Design by Reid Maxim

Author Photo by Joshua Lebovitz Photography

ISBN 9781691292233

Contents

For Peter,
Thank you
and fuck you.

Gravity

The Last

This is the last *fuck you* that I can offer
The one that screams into the night—
Why didn't you pick me?
Why did you let me slip through your fingers like melted ice?
Why wasn't I good enough?
Why didn't you ask, at least once, why is this over?

This is the final plea,
That gravity in the universe will bring you back to me.
Because planets rotate
And moons eclipse,
And I'm not ready to let go of this.

This is the seventh trumpet sounding
Letting the world know the sky is falling,
The end is near
Ring your bell, pack your bag.
The shores will rise to take you away.

This is the final march
The landslide sweeping away the historic remains
The last kiss
Last sleep
Last poem.

Because after this,
There's nothing else.

What I Want From Love

I don't want calm and gentle
Or the kind of love that comes in
When the tide is high
And fades out
With the moon light.
I want earth shattering.
A car accident
And broken glass
That takes weeks to vacuum out.
An aftermath so catastrophic it takes
Months to recover from.
I want gravity that pulls me back
To earth and drowns me in the sea.
I want black coffee
Straight whiskey
And moments that make your breath catch.
So much so I refuse to settle
For calm skies,
Or easy sailing.

December 4, 2014

12:15am

It's a moment, one simple flash where one second he's clumsily shoving my hand away to prevent more pinching, another second where our hands collide, and a flash where they join and the room stops moving.

He doesn't pull away. I keep my eyes straight, focused on the spotlight in front of us. I don't breathe. My heart pounds too hard to hear what is happening on stage.

Does he remember what he told me about holding hands?

I'm careful to keep my fingers completely still. I'm careful not to breathe, think, move, in order to preserve this fragile moment, this flash, one heartbeat longer.

The poet on stage finishes her poem. I never heard her speak. He lets go to clap and the room is in motion again. I follow suit, longing for the warmth that had just encased me.

Before this, my hands had remained in my lap. Now, when I finish my applause, I drop one to the side, his side, and wait.

He doesn't turn to look at me. I don't notice I'm holding my breath until his fingers interlace with mine again, and I exhale a shaky breath.

But holding hands with this boy is like the last breath you take before you get held under water.

I guess it's a good thing I have a good lung span.

Clockwork

I needed you like hours
need minutes.
You were the hand on the clock
pushing things forward, saying
it's okay if this is catastrophe now,
because tomorrow
might be a winning lottery ticket,
a double rainbow day,
a favorite ice cream in summer day.
When the world stood still,
shattered,
you came over picking glass out of my hair,
smoothing out the knots
until the tears dried,
until sanity washed back in.
You were the centerpiece of the world.
My twenty-four hour day
was contingent on your twelve hour hands.
And you,
made the day worth waking up for.

Secrets

This was supposed to be a secret.
The kind where you wake up,
I'm gone,
And we both wonder where the dreams are.

The kind that you tuck safely into envelopes.
Pressed and sealed,
Held together by your tongue.

And yet—
Here we are sitting beside
Each other in a bar.
And you kiss me,
Hard enough to tell your friend
    This is mine
And gently enough to tell me
    I am yours.

But,
This was supposed to be a secret.

So what is it now?

Striking Pavement

He holds my heart the way school children hold rocks.
His arm cocked at any time,
Ready to release.
And though I say he holds this like a rock,
My heart is something more of hand blown glass.
So I know when he lets go,
The world will shatter.
Gravity will pull me down with so much force,
It will set an anchor,
And I will shatter like a windshield in a car accident,
Like the one that killed my best friend.
My heart broke then.
I put it together with masking tape that's not strong enough to hold posters
on painted walls.
I put it together with super glue that washes off hands.
I put it together with duct tape,
With beer bottles,
With putty to fill in the cracks.
I have broken my glass heart so many times,
That maybe this time,
When he throws it and it strikes pavement,
It won't shatter,
It will explode.

Living in Moments

Your fingertips were razorblades
That scarred each place they traced my skin;
The tank top you grazed so gently
I could feel the scabs for years.
I find myself rubbing my chest
Trying to sink you in deeper
Without realizing my hands are moving.
Because when your fingers whispered against me,
My heart listened
And burned lava through my veins in an attempt
To reach you.
To stay in the moment you asked me not to live in.
But your fingertips sliced so softly
I held my breath
Until you tilted my head back,
Matched my lips to yours
And breathed the center of the universe into my lungs.
You tell me not to live in this moment.
But how do you remove yourself
When your heart burst like glitter into starlight?

Breathing Patterns

I learned to breathe in your arms,
pressed against your chest,
your heart setting the tempo.
Two beats in,
two beats out.
Your skin became a compass
used to navigate life;
A bad day meant palms fused together
like two cars in a collision,
metal and shrapnel so intertwined
paramedics couldn't tell my car from yours.
A good day meant finger tips on throats
pressure, patience, and patterned bedsheets that
needed peeled in the morning.
And so it makes sense that when your skin settled into
someone else's,
I was gasping for air.

Replace

My hands were covered in scabs
And bruises
Like a child who had fallen from his bike.
But he, unlike me,
Started with training wheels,
While I began with snow and ice.
You expected me to stay erect,
To pedal forward and not scrape my knees
As I ran from all your late night parties.
Because you'd told me once,
You liked the chase.
But you never warned me,
I'm easy to replace.

I wrote about all those times
So that you would haunt me,
Long after you married her.

The Impermanence of Stars

We hung glow in the dark stars on your ceiling.
I thought it was a sign of permanence,
That with proper constellations,
I would stay until the winter sky came and went.
As it was, the snow was already melting.

We hung glow in the dark stars on your ceiling.
Only these were stickers,
That clung for a bit
And then released their grip, falling to the floor,
The way the rain slapped my car the night you followed me out
To ask me to come back in.

We hung glow in the dark stars on your ceiling,
And I understood that sunlight could spill into a bedroom
When the moon was up,
And be so bright you can't sleep for days.

We hung glow in the dark stars on your ceiling.
We found our zodiac constellations and mapped them out.
I pointed, you peeled,
We hung our universe above our heads.
This one was me,
This one was you.

We hung glow in the dark stars on your ceiling.
When the last one gave in to gravity,
I stood in the door frame of your room
Staring at the empty ceiling.
"Cheer up, kid, we can get others," you said.
So I did.
The plastic ones with putty on the back.

I know they stay because I used them before.
I should have taken the warning.

We hung glow in the dark stars on your ceiling once,
But they were stickers with weak adhesive,
And when they fell,
We never replaced them.

A Small List of Reasons They Left

It isn't fun anymore
I'm interested in your best friend
You're too unstable
I can't handle this
I found someone else and I think this one is going to last a while
I just wanted to be friends (even though I wanted to sleep with you last night)
I think maybe we shouldn't be as good of friends
You deserve better than me
You went to college. You know if you had stayed here, (suffocated yourself, given up everything) we would still be together.

A Small List of Reasons I Left

I'm still waiting for you to come back.

Why We Aren't Together

I assumed that if I listened well enough
If my ears caught the words that rolled off your
Lips and stabbed other girls like dart boards
I could become the target.
But maybe, at the same time,
I'd be the kind of board you hang in your home.
And you said she was too easy,
So for weeks we just kissed on your couch.
Then you said she was too needy,
So I crawled out of bed well before the sun rose and went home.
Then you said this and that
And her and she and they were all wrong.
So I scoured my skin with razorblades to be able to drink enough, be near
enough, pretty enough, while
distant enough.
I scraped my elbows on concrete trying to keep up.
I put band aids on my palms when they broke my fall
From running away after parties.
But then you said,
You preferred brunettes.
So I went home.
I took scissors to my hair with one hand
Hair dye with another.
I took a deep breath,
A diver not quite trusting their oxygen mask.
And set them both down.
Because I was made to believe my hair would have saved me from
concentration camps.
And it was the last piece I couldn't give to you.

Lions and Their Lambs

They said you, Leo
would be protective
of my little lamb heart.

That your muscular body
would curl around mine
and protect me from the winter,
protect me from the loneliness.
Protect me, period.

When you hunted,
I stood to the side, safe on the rocks.
The sunlight clung to you the way water
clings to sand,
the way the stars cling to the sky.

They said you, Leo
and me, Aries
would light the entire world on fire,
and I would be content to watch it all burn.

And we tried,
off and on and off again
constantly in each other's orbit
only an occasional text, phone call,
mountain drive away.

They said the lions look after their lambs.
but they tend to forget
it's so much more common
for the little lamb to be
lead to slaughter.

Leos

He sinks his teeth into me,
canines sharp like lions.
He could adjust,
could find the perfect vein that connects the artery,
could bite down,
and rip it out.

He knows this.
And so he does.

And I stand for thirty seconds,
blood seeping from neck to toe.
A flattering red ribbon dress,
perfectly accentuating my chest,
my thighs,
my life.
And I wonder,
was it worth it,
to have so much hope
that my toothbrush could rest beside his at night?

No

What would have happened if I had stopped running away?
If I had stayed the night you grabbed my arm
As I stormed out of the bar.
What if instead of shrugging you off and telling you to leave it,
I pulled you aside and talked
And finally broke.
Would things have been different?
Would you have stayed,
Rather than moving on to a girl
Whose hair I will spend the rest of my life comparing to?
Because you liked brunettes,
And I'm Holocaust survivor blonde.
Should I have stayed in bed until you woke up,
Instead of creeping out at 5am,
When the sun still slept
And my breath warmed my car faster than the heater?
Would it have made a single difference?
Because you loved to tell me,
That I wasn't good enough,
That I'm not relationship material,
That I am wasted talent,
Because I won't wrap my lips around your dick,
And settling inside me isn't enough for you.
So what if I had stopped running away?
Do you think for a second,
You would have stayed?

Bullet Holes and Band Aids

You weren't a band aid.
You were anesthesia stopping the seizure,
Leather in my mouth so I didn't bite my tongue clean off.
Your firework fingertips cauterized open wounds
That I swore I would bleed to death from.
Bullet holes from another love,
Another life,
That weren't yours to heal.
Your hands completed patchwork quilting
That would put the gods to shame.
You were sunlight in the middle of winter,
The night sky lit, ravenous for sunrise.
You weren't a band aid,
A temporary fix with fun colors that would lose its traction in a day.
You were gravity,
Lips that pressed against scars
And turned them starlight white.
And that is why when you left,
My legs stayed beneath me.

Maybe, Someday, Somewhere

I'm going to give you a universe.
The kind we talked about
where we both say maybe
someday
somewhere.
So that when these worlds collide,
we'll finally know what it's like
to fall asleep together.

Rope Burn

I'm not ready for this.
not ready to open my hand
and let the sand pour out.
I'm not ready to release the string
even though the kite has been away for so long.
Because at least if I held on
I kept it in sight.
I trusted gravity would bring it back down.
But only if I held on.
If I stayed in contact.
So this is happening.
The right step after the left.
The natural order of the world.
And I keep looking ahead
to when the wind steals the sand
takes the kite,
and I'm left on a beach,
with rope burned hands.

What Ifs

You said, you hope I'm not living in the what if's
in the place you left me in.
I tell you I'm not, because
I injected your words like heroin,
so that they entered the blood stream
and circulated in my body for years to come.

All the times you told me I wasn't good enough
I hold in my mouth
a cyanide capsule I bite down on
so that I foam at the edges of my lips
as though I am dehydrated
instead of rabid
as my heart stops beating.

My body cannot hold positive words,
cannot grasp the moments we swapped sunglasses and took a picture
where we smiled
because love looks like that.

My body rubs against these times,
pressed felt fabric that needs to be washed.
But the times you left me crying in a snowbank,
in a parking lot,
in a dimly lit stairwell,
they enter my body.
And so I tell you,
I don't live in the what if's
No, they eat me alive.

The Last Kiss

Maybe I should stay the one that got away,
The one who poured so much of herself
Into you that four years later
I hang from your steering wheel
Like a necklace where your girlfriend can't see.
Ahem.
Your fiancée can't see.
In your phone, you remove all traces of me.
But I still exist in pictures that will never been seen.
I should stay the one who
Cut out her veins
So that your blood could flow better.
And this is why,
After you push me against my car
My heart screams in my ears
My tongue moves in your mouth.
And I dissolve like salt in boiling water.
When we separate,
I stay the one that got away.
And I say,
"Happy marriage."

On Letting Go

I have picked apart my hands
the way birds do road kill,
and like the rotting carcass,
they won't move again.
They will stay to my sides
so that the next time
You/He/They,
reach for me,
they'll grasp the dead air between us.
I will peel back fingernails,
far enough the tips bleed
enough blood that my fingers
stay sensitive,
unlike my heart.
I let the cracks in my skin
splinter and decay
like a door that has been kicked in
because the keys were locked inside.
Only here, there are no keys.
Just empty forests of torn down trees.
You will beg and plead,
and say come back to me.
And I will flash my teeth
because my gums bleed.

On Why This Will Still Hurt

He tells me that it's not a big deal,
That it won't change things.
And I want to tell him,
When I think of the impending moment,
I want to swallow a fifth of vodka with no chaser because it would be easier to
digest.

He tells me I'm overreacting,
Asks me why I say such things.
I want to tell him I want to crawl in a hole that day,
Because he's already tearing the sun out of the sky.
And at least this way,
If I'm already in the dark
I can't see the difference.

He tells me that I'll be okay,
That this really isn't a big deal.
But I spent three years of my life
Winding around him and connecting like strands of DNA
Only to be ripped apart
When he met someone new.
And now he's marrying her.
And he tells me,
It's not a big deal.

Immortal

I figured if I wrote this down
immortalized this through black and white and pen and paper
that when I looked up
my heart would beat differently in my chest.

You see, I thought if I put these words on the outside of my body
that what was left on the inside of me
would stop feeling like insomnia when all I want is to sleep,
would stop feeling like waiting for oxygen when I've been under water for so
long,
would stop....

I thought if I put these words on paper
and you read them the way most people read love letters
your heart would recognize the music
and I would find you at 3am in my parking lot
telling me to put a hoodie on because it's time to go stargazing.
You warned me this would happen as though there were worse things to wake
up to.
So I sleep lighter now.

I thought I could write you out of my system
that what floods out of my being would eventually dry like the wells when
water bottling companies move
in to the town next door.
That I would stop searching for you in the faces of strangers because it feels a
little more like home.

I assumed if I found the right words
this would pour out of me
you would come back to me
and I would stop waking up every time I heard a car door open.

A List of Things I Wish I'd Said

I.
For the first time since my best friend died,
You made time stop in a good way.
I didn't feel like broken glass,
Face peeling off the steering wheel,
Mother begging,
Don't look,
She wouldn't want to see you like this.
For the first time since that time,
I understood why I have eyes.

II.
When I said I liked you,
You responded with, "Why?"
I'm not sure there's a word for the glue that is keeping me together.
Not sure my tongue, my tone, can convey that since you put time in motion,
The mirror has become a friend
Rather than enemy.

III.
You'd said I was taking you home.
Yet, when I went to the bathroom,
I came out and other girls flocked to your side
Because you are gravity and no one can resist your pull.
They were beautiful.
They had long hair,
Their bras perfected their breasts.
And I was wearing skate shoes.
You had me take you home.
Me, over these beautiful, flawless, creatures.
It was the first time I exhaled.

IV.
I wanted, so desperately, to be what you needed.

V.
I dated someone new.
We lived together.
You asked if it was too soon,
And I wondered how long I should have waited for you.

VI.
During a drunken night I
Unbuttoned your pants
Took your debit card
And we got in the one and only screaming match,
Because I wanted you
And not him.

VII.
You said exclusive
But just friends.
I wore a dress to your staff party.
I met your coworkers.
I danced like the end wasn't watching.

VIII.
I laid in your bed when they got engaged.
You said I was okay.
I laid there when they married,
You said I'd be fine.
I was across the country when I told you about my father,
And you said, "I'm sorry, I was trying to figure out what to get for lunch."

IX.
It was raining.
My head was against my steering wheel,
And I cried because you weren't the type to follow me out.
You knocked at my window.

X.
We ended.

XI.
You started dating her the same week.

XII.
Your best friend tells me you're engaged.
He buys me beer at the bar.
You say you didn't mean to hurt me,
That it wouldn't affect me.

XIII.
We're face to face.
We drink beer in front of mutual friends.
You push me against my car,
And when we separate, you're still planning a wedding.

XIV.
You invite me to the bachelor party.
Rather, the party after the party.
To your hotel room.
We fall asleep holding hands.
My head is on your chest.
And you tell me you're happy with her.

XV.
You marry her,
On the anniversary of my best friend's burial.
I'm not invited to the wedding.

To My Almost Ex On His Wedding Day

I hope her hands continue to feel soft and warm
Because mine are always cold, and sometimes cracked.

I hope when you promise in sickness, in health, in aging,
Her hair stays brunette for several more years
Because you hated my blonde
And God knows how you'll handle grey.

I hope when you fall asleep at night,
Her head rests like a cloud against your shoulder
Rather than an anchor dragging you down.

I hope that when you stand alone
Buttoning your tux
Checking your hair in the mirror another time
My phantom doesn't haunt the background
Like it did in your hotel room.

I hope that when you say forever
Someday, you actually mean it.

I hope her dress fits perfectly,
Her make up is spot on,
And when you see her walking down the aisle,
Rather than shed a tear of joy,
Your hands shake in panic.

I hope that when the photographer takes the picture,
Your smiles stretch so far a planet could throw up in your mouth.

I hope that when people see the photos,
They comment how happy you are,

Because they don't see when the make up slides off.

I hope that when you look at your phone
Your heart still skips a beat when you see my name.
Only, it won't read as my name, will it?
Because she doesn't know we stayed in touch
Or take note of your hand in your pocket.

I hope that you discover what happiness is
Because it isn't this.

I Wish I Had Listened

The time we sat at the bar
And another girl approached and left
You laughed with your friends.
You boasted about how much she wanted you
About how you had her before.
I should have listened to the way you'd peel my clothes like skin from a chicken,
Leave me like the girl you boasted about.

The time you told me
I wasn't the type you'd want to date
That I wasn't good enough for you
As though I should have submitted a better resume
Instead of sharing three years of couches, beds,
Sneaking off after the bar patrons dwindled.

The time you told me you preferred brunettes
And you met her
While we weren't dating
But we were exclusive.
I ripped open my chest
Told you secrets I rarely share
Only to be met with static silence.
There were words, but they were empty.

The time you told me
About all of the other girls
The one you "skull fucked"
The one you led on
The one you burned through like a forest fire so that her ashes wiped all over
me when I laid in your bed.

I am all of these girls
And they
Are me.
And you, my darling boy
Who will never grow up
Who will kiss girls while engaged
Spend nights with girls after a bachelor party
Who tucks his hand in his pocket
When posing beside his wife,
You, boy
Are not good enough for me.

To Make You Love Me

I should not have to plead to you,
to cut off my hair,
bleach it,
color it darker,
to get you to see me.

I should not have to scream
so that your head turns in my direction.

I should not gut myself
with my own knives
and wait, bleeding on the floor
until you come back to me.

I should not,
but I would have.
And I will not.

Now.

Notes

The following poems appear in *Gravity* with thanks to their initial publishers:

"Breathing Patterns," *Back Patio Press*

"The Impermanence of Stars," *Storm of Blue Press*

"Leos," *Cauldron Anthology*, They Who Were Spurned

"On Letting Go," *Frost Meadow Review*, Volume 2

"To Make You Love Me," *Crêpe & Penn*, Issue No. 2

Acknowledgements

I want to thank whoever is holding this book in their hands. Thank you for taking your time and investing in my project, my writing. It means more to me than I can express and with your consent, I would like to give you a hug. (If yes here's a ::Hug::, if not, here's a solid high five.)

This project and so much of my writing has too many people supporting me in the background. It's likely that I'm going to forget some folks, so I'm sorry in advance. I'll just leave it at – thank you to anyone who has ever edited or supported my work while it was underground. Thank you to those who have come to my readings, snapped, or clapped at the end.

First and foremost, thank you Peter – this collection would not have lived without you. Thank you for being the center of the universe for the time you were, for pushing me to become better, and for helping in all the ways you have.

Thank you to Alex Ruiz who pushes my poetry to the level it can be, even if it hurts my feelings or if I'm cursing at the computer screen after all the edits. You make my work better, and I am so grateful for it.

Maya Williams and the Quill Books and Beverage writing group for reigniting my want to write and sustaining me for an entire Summer and Fall. I would have been lost and given up without the encouragement from the writing group. Thank you for your ears and your eyes, and the tremendous amounts of support. Shout out to Courtney MacMunn Schlachter at Quiet City Books for giving me space to share my work on so many occasions.

And in no particular order: thank you Jessie Tweedie, Patrick McDonald, and Emily Robinson for usually being the first set of eyes on my work. Gabrielle Byrne for pushing me to not give up, and occasionally kicking me to get back on the writing horse when I'd rather throw a fit. Also, Holly Moyseenko –

you once told me I'm the living Sylvia Plath and my writing has been thriving because of that energy since.

Speaking of support, nothing I do would be possible without the help of Mary Penet and Chris Penet. Thank you for being my rocks, my sounding board, and the adult voice when I don't know where else to turn. You're the best family a girl could ask for.

Thank you to Juliette and *Nightingale and Sparrow* for believing in my work. There are not enough words to convey my gratitude so I guess just read the Twitter threads. I wouldn't have trusted my first collection with anyone else.

Lastly, thank you to my mom – for listening to me read poetry to you for hours on end, offering feedback, helping arrange the order of various poems, and your support.

About the Author

Lynne Schmidt is a mental health professional in Maine who writes memoir, poetry, and young adult fiction. Her unpublished memoir, *The Right to Live: A Memoir of Abortion* received the 2018 Maine Nonfiction Award and was a 2018 PNWA finalist, while her poetry received the Editor's Choice Award for her poem, Baxter, from *Frost Meadow Review* and was a 2019 PNWA finalist. She is a five-time Best of the Net 2019 nominee and the founder of AbortionChat (@AbortionChat on Twitter), where she does presentations on the intersections of mental health, writing,  and reproductive justice. When given the option, she prefers the company of her three dogs and one cat to humans.

Find Lynne on Twitter @lynneschmidt and on her Facebook page, Lynn(e) Schmidt.

If you enjoyed *Gravity*....

Consider leaving a review on Amazon, Goodreads, or your favourite website (or tell a friend!).

Recommend or donate a copy to your local library.

Try one of our previously published titles or an issue of our literary magazine and stay tuned for these upcoming publications from Nightingale & Sparrow Press:

Cemetery Music by Birdy Odell (December 2019)

Dichotomy by Mikhayla Robinson (March 2020)

A Daughter for Mr. Spider by Megan Russo (April 2020)

Heal My Way Home by Rachel Tanner (October 2020)

What Lasts Beyond the Burning by A.A. Parr (December 2020)

Pandora by Mollie Williamson (April 2021)

Keep up to date with *Nightingale & Sparrow*:

nightingaleandsparrow.com

Facebook: /nightingaleandsparrow
Twitter: @nightandsparrow
Instagram: @nightingaleandsparrow

Nightingale
& Sparrow
PRESS

Made in the USA
Middletown, DE
05 February 2023

23943389R00035